AD WAMMES

T0086959

FIDUCIE

MUSIC DEPARTMENT

OXFORD
UNIVERSITY PRESS

*Offered to the Protestantse wijkgemeente Rotterdam-Schiebroek by the Rev. Rik Radstake
in celebration of his fortieth anniversary as a minister on 26 August 2018*

Fiducie

AD WAMMES

I: Principal 8', Flute 8'
II: Principal 8', Flute 8'
III: Flutes 8', 4', Oboe 8'
Pedal: Flute 16', Principal 8', I/Ped.

The first performance was given by Iddo van der Giessen on 26 August 2018 at the Goede Herderkerk Rotterdam-Schiebroek.

© Oxford University Press 2021

Printed in Great Britain

OXFORD UNIVERSITY PRESS, MUSIC DEPARTMENT, GREAT CLARENDON STREET, OXFORD OX2 6DP
The Moral Rights of the Composer have been asserted. Photocopying this copyright material is ILLEGAL.

4